GW00492659

With Warmest Best Wishes from
Maureen Cahalan

A New Beginning

When the daily challenges of life have no meaning; when eating, working, thinking or even dressing yourself seems unimportant anymore, then it's time to grasp the magnitude of the moment and prepare ourselves for a better life - little by little, day by day, moment by moment. With time, agony and anxiety turn to hope and with hope comes freedom to see who we are and what we have. We are all made to feel uniquely different; therefore, our way of coping with change is unique to ourselves. Out of apathy we will find the light and with the light we can ground ourselves to find a better way of life. Separation from work or a loved one does not end life; it creates an opportunity for new life. We will find new meaning for ourselves to move forward, without the shadows of isolation, hurt or anxiety. Life is about living, growing and giving.

Without mental or physical health, life is not life. Come walk with me on a healing journey within, for renewed hope, activity and inspiration.

Carve your own identity for yourself in your own time. Deal with emotions and focus their energies positively. Lean on resources available to you. Understand yourself and your inner strengths. Follow the step-by-step process of healing for renewed energy. Reconcile from within and take control of your life. Prepare yourself for a new beginning to live through new eyes; reinvent every part of you. Make a commitment to yourself that you will do something meaningful every day.

The Winds of Change blow Gently Across all our Lives

Getting More Out of Life

Getting more out of life doesn't necessarily happen at the speed we expect. Retirement or separation are not destinations. With bereavement, there is a full stop; with retirement or separation there is a comma. The hurt, pain, suffering and turmoil each destination creates is a different experience for everybody. However, we must reach a destination and prepare ourselves for our own onward journey. The timing of this journey depends on us. My hope is that this book will guide you to the right frame of mind, by replacing the hurt, fear or anxiety within you with the beginning of a more welcoming future.

For me, something was missing and I could not put my finger on it. I now realise that I was spending too much time wondering why this was. The day I woke up to the fact that success and happiness in life depended completely on myself, my own motivation and determination to move forward with my life was born. Without knowing, I am preparing myself for retirement too.

Firstly, I gave myself permission to smile. The day I heard myself laugh out loud was the day I started to recover. It was the most healthy, hopeful and positive sign and sound that I had experienced for four years.

I know now that I have travelled a long and bumpy journey. By allowing positive help to enter my life from being open to new opportunities and from a support group, I have learned to cope. I'm certainly not as fearful or as lonely as I was in the early days. To reach this point was hard work and I continue to work on it and with it every day of my life.

The Power Within us is Greater than the Struggle we Face

Stages of Heartache

Sorrow, grief and hurt can educate us hugely on life's journey. The belief that we can see further through a tear than through a telescope may comfort us in the knowledge that we are human and fragile. The power within us is greater than the challenge ahead of us. We must believe that as children of the universe, we will get through our pain and suffering. I do not like the term grief; I find it too clinical. The word heartache is more descriptive because what we are going through is heartache which, if allowed, can tear us into tiny pieces. Our focus needs to be on mending the ache and to begin to see things differently - albeit slowly and over time.

The main stages of heartache and hurt are:

- Shock or disbelief
- Denial
- Bargaining
- Guilt
- Anger
- Depression
- Acceptance and hope

Stages of Heartache

We will see some, if not all, of the main stages of heartache and hurt as we grieve and cope due to the loss of a relationship. It will not ease the pain but it does help to understand what we are going through. Time is the best healer of all sorrows. We are never fully healed, but we have to have the belief that it becomes easier to manage, allowing ourselves to move forward on our onward journey.

- The first stage of shock or disbelief comes when we are faced with hearing the news of a death or loss of a relationship. We quite naturally are propelled into turmoil and find the seriousness of the situation difficult to take in. It leaves us numb, detached and confused.

- Denial is another stage of the heartache process and sometimes this stage will last only a moment, while with others, it can play on the mind for quite some time.

- Each of the main stages of heartache will take different lengths of time to work through from person to person. Sometimes, the first stages may only last a moment and with others, they could last for a considerable period of time.

- Bargaining is trying to negotiate something within ourselves; it is something we do to protect our sanity and logical way of thinking. We might say, 'What could I have done to prevent the loss?', 'Why me?' or 'Why has this happened to me?'. This is quite natural and is an observed stage of our heartache and coping mechanism.

The Power Within us is Greater than the Struggle we Face

Stages of Heartache

+ The guilt then starts to raise its head, and can sometimes feel a bit like bargaining. We tend to blame ourselves in an effort to reconcile the loss or ending of the relationship. We build up a list of reasons why this has happened, and start beating ourselves up.

+ When anger occurs in the heartache process, we're actually beginning to move forward. All of the stages up to this one have been very inward reactions, whereas anger is more of an outward emotion, which is designed to heal our pain.

+ Depression is not so much a stage; it can be continuous throughout the whole heartache process. When the anger stage has passed, depression will also become less and less and we will start to feel more in control.

+ Finally, acceptance and hope will return and marks the breakthrough stage of our heartache. At this point we understand that life will never be the same, but we will see hope for the future.

+ The main stages of heartache should be understood in the context of what's happening to us. We all react differently to the different stages, and deal with them in our own time, in our own way.

The Winds of Change blow Gently Across all our Lives

Love for ourselves is understanding
the beauty of who we are

Eternal hope lives gently
in the human heart

The Power Within us is Greater than the Struggle we Face

What I have learned about myself in recent years

+ Believing I was young and strong and I would get over it; but looking back, I don't think I wanted to get over it.

+ Following the heartache, I slowly began to wake up with feelings of hope that I might have a future. I began to balance despair with hope, tears with laughter and bad times with good.

+ Came to accept the changes that separation has brought to my life. I am open to new experiences and I know now that I have a future.

+ Learning that when you love somebody, they never fully leave you.

+ Acknowledging that death is not separate from life and I am no longer frightened by it.

+ Understanding that grief is like a journey - I had to be very patient, understanding and kind to myself along the way.

+ Accepting that I needed to grieve in my own way, and that nobody else could fully understand what it was like for me.

The Winds of Change blow Gently Across all our Lives

Facing the ending of a relationship

This is a difficult task which can only be worked on by ourselves (but we can seek help!)

The two ways of dealing with it:

+ Avoid the challenge and stay the same

  Or

+ Look directly at the problem and analyse it

+ Familiarise yourself with the concept and take each day at a time.
+ Accept that there is a reason for everything.
+ Take the focus back to ourselves.
+ Create a psychological contract with yourself that you will be in control, not to be controlled.
+ Reach out and help others who are less fortunate; this takes inner strength but will strengthen our resolve.
+ Break-ups, natural death, sudden death, accidental death and partings from our families propel us into a world of numbness and pain. We need time to heal and give ourselves permission to heal.
+ We need to learn to control this numbness rather than be controlled by it.
+ The love and warmth around us needs to be slowly welcomed by ourselves.

What helped me along the way

- People in my life who simply listened with patience and respect to what I had to say. People who did NOT try to make me feel better. Attract the right people into your life.

- Allowing yourself and giving yourself the freedom to have a bad day at any time - but to get over it too.

- Going for long walks in the heart of the country or beside the sea.

- I was told that grief and loneliness had 7 stages. I disagree with that; it may even have 77 or 777 stages. Now I know that it does not follow any set course or pattern.

- There is no right way to make this journey and no right amount of time it should take.

- With care, support and understanding you can learn to adapt to make it manageable.

- Losing a partner, sibling or child can feel overwhelming, particularly in the first two or three years. There comes a point when we are ready for our onward journey to recovery. This will allow ourselves to take our place in the world.

The Winds of Change blow Gently Across all our Lives

Negative Human Emotions

Here is a list of negative human emotions. The purpose is to be in control of them and not be controlled by them.

- Sadness
- Emptiness
- Loneliness
- Pain
- Insecurity
- Envy
- Despair
- Feeling of hopelessness
- Impatience
- Worry
- Irritation
- Bad humour
- Lack of energy

The Power Within us is Greater than the Struggle we Face

Positive Human Emotions

By replacing negative human emotions or behaviours with positive ones, we are making a deliberate effort to regain our positivity and value as a beautiful human being. Each emotion is within our grasp, but it takes effort to change our way of thinking and doing.

- *Patience*
- *Serenity*
- *Peace*
- *Joy*
- *Love*
- *Forgiving*
- *Giving*
- *Helpfulness*
- *Gentleness*
- *Calmness*
- *Understanding*
- *Clarity*
- *Energy*

The Winds of Change blow Gently Across all our Lives

Negative Behaviour **attracts** Negative Behaviour = **Negative Feeling**

Negative Behaviour **influenced by** Positive Behaviour = **Positive Feeling**

Negative behaviour is easier to accept. Positive behaviour is harder to embrace, yet from experience we know that it is more rewarding for us.

The Power Within us is Greater than the Struggle we Face

Striving to our potential

Each one of us should feel and realise that we have great potential. With self-confidence, more positivity and a little more effort, we can change if we want to. When we feel that our present way of life is unpleasant or difficult, then let us try not to look at those negatives. We need to see the positive side, the potential and make an effort to change our way of thinking. The main source of a happy life comes from within. Try to minimise and delete those negative emotions, thoughts and memories. Try from this time onward to allow our MAIN INTEREST to be that which will create a happier us.

Learning from People around us

I have learned over the past few years that I am not independent of others. My happiness depends on others' happiness too. When I meet and see and hear from happy people, I automatically feel happier. Despite all of this, I have to be honest and tell you that mental transformation takes time and is not easy. For me, it has taken two to four years; for others it can take from three months to five years, but it's well worth working at it. Make a constant effort to work at it every day and you will eventually find some wonderful and happy changes.

People Attraction

We tend to have greater liking for those who like us and are therefore more attracted to people who display approval for our actions. The belief that other people like us affects the way we behave, making our actions more fulfilling. So by being nice to all people, this will be helpful to both them and ourselves… and always wear a smile.

It's Natural to feel isolated… but with effort we can change to embrace

- Fear of being left alone…light a candle, soft music, warms the room
- Not looking forward to long evenings…plan your time
- Not socialising…take one step at a time, even a trip to the shop
- Avoiding people…seek out positive people, do a good turn
- Loss of memory…buy a little note book and write notes
- Forgetting peoples' names…smile and be gentle
- Living with memories…focus on the quality rather than quantity
- Being reminded by pictures…reduce number of reminders
- Don't be too hard on yourself…make a list - there is always another day
- Over-doing too many things…have daily downtime

The Winds of Change blow Gently Across all our Lives

On Being Yourself

You must learn that you cannot be loved by all people. You can be the finest apple in the world - ripe, juicy, sweet, succulent - and offer yourself to all. But you must remember that there will be people who do not like apples. You must understand that if you are the world's finest apple, and someone you love does not like apples, you have the choice of becoming a banana. But you must be warned that if you choose to become a banana, you will be a second-rate banana. But you can always be the finest apple. You must also realise that if you choose to be a second-rate banana, there will be people who do not like bananas. Furthermore, you can spend your life trying to become the best banana - which is impossible if you are an apple - or you can seek again to be the finest apple.

Author unknown

Forgiveness

We must make a decision to be reconciled with all the people in our lives. Decide to set them free and in so doing, we set ourselves free too. Life is too short and too precious for us to waste it being bound up in the strings and chains of unnecessary feelings of hurt. We must let it go. Forgiveness takes time; it takes maturity. Forgiveness is a choice. When we decide to forgive, we decide to move forward with our lives.

Releasing ourselves from the bonds that grip us and make peace within ourselves creates new life. We must do it to free ourselves up for the positive things in life.

We can't control what other people did, do, said or say to us but we can decide to create peace of mind through forgiveness. The time will come for us to stop wasting time and energy on what is beyond our control, instead, we can decide to be in a better place.

Forgiveness starts with a decision - the emotion, reward and feeling the sense of happiness will follow.

Happiness

Happiness takes personal effort and sacrifice - it is not easy. Happiness is beautiful, infectious and unifying. We deserve to be happy. We deserve to create a newer, more self assured us. To use our magical sparkle to influence those we meet with positivity and openness is everlasting.

Let's be Honest Here...

+ Change can be very damaging when it's external.
+ We need to accept and embrace change internally; this takes time
+ With time comes hope and with hope comes faith in ourselves.
+ We must believe that there is a greater reason.
+ We must strive to believe that things will come right.

+ I should have sought help earlier in my grief, loneliness and loss.
+ I allowed negativity to control me. Looking back on it now, I would not wish anybody to go through the same experience.
+ We should have one purpose - to learn how to be happy.
+ Let each of us carry the light in the comfort and hope that our light will shine.

The Power Within us is Greater than the Struggle we Face

Love is patient, Love is kind.
It does not envy, it does not boast, it is not proud.
It is not rude, it is not self-seeking, it is not easily angered,
It keeps no record of wrongs.
Love does not delight in evil but rejoices with the truth.
It always protects, always trusts, always hopes, always preserves.

Love is eternal

Daily tips that work for me which I feel are worth sharing

- Start each day with a positive thought
- Drink plenty of water at room temperature
- Smile every day (whether I have something to smile about or not)
- Watch my diet carefully in a relaxed, disciplined approach
- Take daily down time in a relaxed setting
- Interact with positive people
- Stay clear of time thieves
- Learn something new about myself daily
- End each day with appreciation and a positive thought

A jewel of wisdom for you is to mentally gear yourself to enjoy nature or have an equal alternative. Don't just think about it.

Plan it, do it and enjoy it.

Come The Dawn

After a while, you learn the difference
Between holding a hand and chaining a soul
And you learn that love does not mean security
And you begin to learn that kisses are not contracts
And presents are not promises
And you begin to accept your defeats
With your head up and your eyes open
With the grace of an adult, not the grief of a child
And you learn to build all your roads today
Because tomorrow's ground
Is too uncertain for plans, and futures have
A way of falling down in mid-flight
After a while you learn that even sunshine
Burns if you get too much
So you plant your own garden and decorate
Your own soul instead of waiting
For someone to bring you flowers
And you learn that you really can endure
That you really are strong
And you really have worth

Author unknown

Healing ourselves is like painting a new canvas of ourselves

- Develop awareness of what you want to change about you
- Concentrate on what and who is important in your life
- Positive self-talk is really important
- Have a positive relationship with yourself
- Have a healthy lifestyle
- Be open to opportunities
- Engage in open and interesting communication
- Avoid getting involved in unnecessary conversations
- Let most of what you hear over your head
- Avoid taking things personally
- We can attract and hold onto positive people in our life
- Remember, everything in moderation - including people!

The Power Within us is Greater than the Struggle we Face

Kiss Your Ass Good Bye

One day a granddad and his very young grandson set off with their donkey. The Granddad rode the donkey and the child walked trying to keep up with them. They met people who said "That is so cruel having that child walking and running with a fine strong man being carried by the ass." So they exchanged places and now the young boy was being carried by the ass. They met another group of people who said "that is so cruel and unfair to have your grandfather walking and a healthy young boy being carried by the ass." So the two of them decided that they'd both mount the donkey and he would carry them. On turning the corner they met another group of people who said "that is so cruel to the donkey - 2 people being carried by him."The two got down and each put a front leg of the donkey on their shoulder and tried to carry the ass. As they crossed the bridge the donkey fell into the river and drowned, so the morale of the story is "If you try to please all people you can kiss your ass good bye."

" *When you change for the better, you allow others change for the better too. In changing you become a role model and people will automatically see the value you have as a person.*"

Always be in control...

What you say

What you don't say

What you do

How you do it

The Winds of Change blow Gently Across all our Lives

It's Time to Celebrate Me

I am celebrating me today. I am worth it. I am an unique individual and there is only ever going to be one of me. With all my worth, individuality, talents, love and potential…it is time for me, I am an unique creation.

My place cannot be taken for I am here. The hand that made me, carved my uniqueness and my spirit. My destiny is within my reach. Believing in myself with love, attention, care and developing myself will allow my light to shine in this world. I am me and I belong here, I am a child of the universe who was born out of love and light.

It matters not, where I have come from, it only matters where I am going. By loving myself, I allow the world to see me and love me for who I am. I cannot control what other people do or say or what they have done. I can decide not to feel being victimised or to stop wasting time and energy, Instead, I can decide to strive for something better. There is something inside so strong which I cannot deny. I am me.

The spirit inside me is a flame waiting to ignite. I want my light to shine.

Today I am celebrating me. I take my place in the world with new energy, new life and new hope. I am here to make a difference, to allow myself grow. Letting go of the past, forgiving people and myself, this allows me to move from the past into the present. I am not alone; time has come to celebrate me.

Life was given to me. Hope was given to me. Like a sunrise or the light of the moon…with gentleness, today, I celebrate me.

Maureen Cahalan

Rest a While

Rest is not inactivity, it is an activity
There is a great need for us to slow down,
We all need time out to enjoy
physical, emotional, psychological and
spiritual rest.

The Road in the Sky

There is always a road in the sky for those who seek it,

There is always a road in the sky for those who want it,

Signposts may be invisible,

Landmarks indistinguishable

But the road is there.....if we allow ourselves to look for it.

The Three Symbols

You are my past, my present and my future

By offering up my thoughts, feelings and emotions,
I allow my mind be open to change, encourage new energy
within me and the spirit which is me connects me with love

Chartering New Opportunities

We are all as one, humanity connects us in a way
that is as beautiful as it is fascinating. The slow winds of
change gently cross all our lives. We need to seek new
life and opportunities with the changing world we live in.

Looking out for You

Dear Tom,

Recently I met a friend who shared with me the lovely news that you are retiring soon. I hope that you are taking things in your stride. I can assure you that you will be amazed at the new adventure life is offering you. There is no time for unnecessary worries. Since I retired about 3 years ago, I thought that I would share my experience with you. The first few weeks were quite a novelty not having to get up in the morning and watch the clock. Then I started planning things to do. Going on holiday every year since retirement has given me new energy. I never went on holiday before but the feeling of not having to return to work was beautiful.

Spending time in the garden is my little piece of heaven, growing my own vegetables for the first time in my life is wonderful. There are various active retirement groups in the community which are great for meeting people. Being with like minded people is terrific . Please give me a call when it suits you, I would welcome a chat and maybe we can discuss things that are common to us both.

Until we meet, Jack

Home Coming to bygone days

I felt immediately I had to go home, home is homeland and hometown. Sitting in the foyer of the hotel that evening sipping wine I felt more at ease than I had done for months. I was back in my country where I always preferred the pace of life, the laughter, the friendliness, and yes the singing and dancing. Best of all was hearing the Irish accent. I love to hear it here in England, but when I return to Ireland it is so infectious I begin to hear myself falling back into Irish sayings, pronunciations etc. I say 'Weren't you great' and laugh inwardly at myself.

The day after my arrival I hired a car and made my way down the country to Swinford, my hometown. The roads had improved but still there was the feeling of driving through the country, passing through small towns, past farms and lush green fields. The thatched cottages maybe gone but are replaced with charming modern bungalows. As I approached Swinford I saw the landmark church on the hill.

The shops had hardly changed. There was still the haunting smell of bacon and sausages. My favourite items to this day are Irish rashers, as the Irish say, sausages, black pudding and white pudding, but above all Irish butter. How I missed those items of food when I left Ireland in 1959. I went into one of the many bars for a coffee. The kettle was put on and immediately it felt so good to have a tenderly made cup of coffee, not some machine produced variety of coffee. I got back into the car and drove the mile out of town to the farm where I was born. I drove over the railway crossing and swung down the boithrin (country lane) to an embankment by the river, a tributary of the Shannon which ran through the farm. I felt a stranger, which saddened me deeply, especially as I was born there, in the bungalow that had been built in 1935 for my grandmother by her children who had gone off to England and America to better themselves.

As I left the farmland, I made my way to the main road and took the eight mile drive to Knock. For the rest of my life this place will call me back and answer all my prayers, as it has done since I first visited as a very young child. In times of trouble a place can have great meaning. As I sat there I felt totally at peace in myself, which was another source of strength for me.

My trip to Ireland and the memories it evoked has helped me make great strides in my life. I knew I needed the determination of my grandmother and mother, the courage to make it as they had shown courage through many hardships. To have courage is so important and you learn that it can even be acquired when you have the love of your family, inner will; future vision and a willingness to embrace new challenges and all those you meet in life. Sometimes you have to make that big entrance on your own, but once you do you will find that people applaud your bravery, you can become a hero to someone more timid than you. You have to be the best actress even though you are dying inside. If I wanted to I could curl up and die. I owe it to myself to do the best I can do in the time that I can do it.

O.E.

A Letter for a Dear Friend

Dear Joan,

Delighted to hear that you are getting ready to retire from work , I want to wish you the best of good luck, health and happiness and enjoy the rest of your life. It can be a magical time of new opportunities and challenges. We all have the hills and hollows but you are not alone.

I found retiring great for many reasons but with the changes it brings, it takes about 3 months to fully adjust. You will need to manage your time; do things that you have always wanted to do but didn't have time for e.g visit friends and new acquaintances. Keep up some of your friendships with work mates every other month, in this way the change will not be as daunting and believe me in six months you won't want to hear about the work load. Taking up a hobby like golf, walking or gardening or a little of everything until you find your niche. It is most definitely worth the effort. My all important message is to keep active outside and inside the house.

With much love, Kay

Heart of Ireland Focus Groups…Making the Change

Knowing what to do and actually doing it makes all the difference on the journey towards happiness. Remember, 'What you've always done is now done and life is presenting a golden opportunity to do things differently!' Here is some of the learning from the focus groups…

Being part of a group is so important

Developing your personal skills

Active awareness

Beautiful message of being active in retirement

Very informative, clear and fulfilling

Time management with people too!

Really listening to people is very important

How not to interrupt people wins relationships

Being aware of how to phrase sentences to get a fruitful conversation

New approach to life gave me a new confidence for life

Not to assume that everybody knows what I am thinking or talking about

Power of being positive and making an effort is worth it

The Winds of Change blow Gently Across all our Lives